Open Door, Open Wall

poems

Greg Watson

Open Door, Open Wall

Second Edition
Copyright © 2020 Greg Watson
All rights reserved.

Originally published in 1998 as a chapbook
by
Malevolence Publications

<u>Credits</u>
Cover Photo: Pixabay
Author Photo: Jordana Torgeson
Layout: Vida Raine

ISBN13: **9798681904427**

Acknowledgements

"Clean" previously appeared in
Poetry Forum and *Invisible Ink*.

"Because" previously appeared in
Newsletter Inago.

"Waiting for Dreamtime," "Summer's End," and "A Very
Brief War Poem" previously appeared in
Naugahyde Literary Journal.

"Muse" previously appeared in
Djinni.

"Stem" previously appeared in
Kumquat Meringue.

"View from a Lonely Room" previously appeared in
Naugahyde Literary Journal, and *Tight*.

"There was Rain" previously appeared in
Muse of Fire, and *blood & feathers*.

"Moon Necklace" previously appeared in
5th Gear.

"And One for my Painter Friend" previously appeared in
Dream International Quarterly.

"Dream of an Ohio Opera" previously appeared in
Dream International Quarterly, and *Tight*.

"Red Ribbon" previously appeared in
Tight.

"Lullaby" previously appeared in
blood & feathers.

"The Poet," "Whiskey Days," and "Landlocked"
previously appeared in
Orbis.

Open Door, Open Wall was the winner of the
1998 *blood & feathers* Chapbook Series Contest,
and was originally published by
Malevolence Publications.

Titles by Greg Watson

All the World at Once: New and Selected Poems

What Music Remains

The Distance Between Two Hands

Things You Will Never See Again

Pale Light from a Distant Room

Cold Water Memory

Annmarie Revisions

Open Door, Open Wall

Many titles available from Nodin Press

www.NodinPress.com

Other Contributions

The Road by Heart: Poems of Fatherhood

Edited by Greg Watson and Richard Broderick

published by Nodin Press

CONTENTS

CLEAN

I will scour my mind
stubbornly, until
it has returned
to its original muck,
place where only
a lotus could grow.

BECAUSE

Because I cry when I hear a train whistle
and words travel too slowly,
I am lonely today.

Because I am attached to form,
I long for your body next to mine,
every wonder and mistake of the flesh
to take to bed and hold.

Because the world is water
and you and I are water, the bodies
beneath our own
become the only life rafts
that we can claim,
the only hold we know.

Because I do not swim, I drown
in measured ways daily:
in sleep, while walking, talking, musing,
as the wine of daylight flows
and fades away.

Because I write to a self
I do not yet know or understand,
I am a man accustomed
to waiting.

I am not afraid to drown.
I do not move away.

SUMMER'S END

The cat's dish is covered with cobwebs;
the sky, more ancient than usual,
cracks at the corners like a lost painting
discovered in an attic
after the war, its edges beginning
to peel, beginning to curl
like the wired spring
of an all-encompassing scroll.
Today is no one's birthday,
and it tells you so.
The terror of summer leaves
is the terror of waking
and finding blueberries instead of knuckles:
a new season has awakened
and left you asleep
in the steps of passing strangers.
You throw your hands up and wait,
not knowing who or what for.

MUSE

It had been
so long
since you entered
the room that
way — as sudden
and slender
as your smile,
the air smoldering
with the immediacy
of the infinite,
words and poems
dripping from
your sleeves,
as if your shadow
had taken
leave simply
to sing its song
to me.

STEM

There's a tulip
where the stem of
your body
once stood,
shot out of itself
into the shock
of daylight,
a familiar sugar
lingering
in an otherwise
empty field:
and like a hand
waving
slowly, slowly,
no one else
notices
the scent
or the persistence
of the form
left behind.

A VERY BRIEF WAR POEM

1.
The uniform in the closet
still bears the shape
of the man.

The boots down at the thrift store
are caked in layers of
fine, white dust.

2.
Night after night,
the white moth batters against
the mesh of window screen,
charging toward
a distant homeland of light.
Reason has no authority here.
Neither of us understand
why we do what we do;
neither of us will know peace until
long into the night.

VIEW FROM A LONELY ROOM

This room is too large
for one set of lungs, too lazy
to get up and walk away,
the unpainted wood of dumb furniture
stretched into the ordinary;
mail and magazines
stamped with coffee cup moons
scattered around
bits of half-finished poems,
all busy and content to discuss
their lives, old and new,
as the typewriter — museum piece —
hums like a second breath,
buzzes and purrs like a furnace
full of words, hungry
for bone and for thought
and for memory
I simply cannot offer today.

THE LONG ROAD

There is a road unseen
that leads away from this window,
an endless ribbon
that no one else may know.
It goes wherever you go,
follows the light between our words.
When I am without,
I need only begin walking.
It has always been this way.

THERE WAS RAIN

There was rain
        dripping from
your fingertips
        that evening in
the park like
        honey like serum
from an Easter
        lily and I was
thirsty I was
        so thirsty.

POEM OF SILENCE

I am writing of the white light bulb
reflected in the black window,
of an old friend
two thousand miles away, as if
we were two hermits on separate mountains
considering the same moon.
There is a rain, though not quite
a rain, people conversing
from apartment balconies like lazy auctioneers.
Occasionally an automobile passes
with the indifferent disturbance
of wind through trees, black flash of tires
leaving no trace in their wake.
I'm writing to say that I am content
with these things, with what passes
for silence in this city — distant strains of
off-kilter jazz, tough-minded crows
caw-cawing for the early kill,
heat pipes wheezing like an old asthmatic
woman who never quite makes it
up the stairs to my door.

MOON NECKLACE

Alone in the loneliness of Mississippi,
the moon leaks in like the fat
off buttermilk, black creepers clamor
the windowsill to drink.

From the gravy-thick darkness,
bullfrogs belch like bloated livers,
weeping willows drag their wild, sleepy-time
hair across long-forgotten graves.

The night sleeps beside you undisturbed,
a thousand dreams I wish I could be —
jewelry, glasses, books, thoughts unfinished
angled along the bedside in silence.

I will leave this poem at your feet
in the morning. I can't wait for breakfast.

AND ONE FOR MY PAINTER FRIEND

I dreamed you were selling your paintings
at the off-ramp of the freeway,
some still damp, hanging
from the lamp posts and chain-link fence.
Your horn-rimmed glasses hung
like safety scissors,
one side of your face evading cones of light,
your hair unkempt and knotted
with encaustic wax.
Cones of light from vehicles swam past
with neither sound nor interest,
lighting up your cities and rivers,
your tangled forests,
impossible to enter or to leave;
impossible to tell where one scene ended
and another began.
You did not notice me.
I was the crow swooping down
for a random scrap of cellophane,
lingering for a moment
to catch a better view.

WAITING FOR DREAMTIME

The worms are sweating olive oil
in the unrelenting heat,
day-crawlers awaiting the rain
to wash them into long tangles of prayer
leading back into the earth.
A twenty-pound cat stretches under
the canopy of an ash tree;
a white moth made of gauze
lands on one leaf, then another,
flutters like a lost thought.
The day drones on without argument.

THE ANSWER

It came too late,
as answers
often do;
but like an old
box of nails
he kept it around
for future use,
that long rainy day
when the same
questions
would inevitably
return, at once.

ALL NIGHT THE SAME MOTH

All night the same moth
fluttering against
the broken window screen.
I could go on and on,
chasing it back into the waiting
darkness, neither of us
learning a thing.

PASTORAL

Then the postman arrived with the month
of November, everything
suddenly gray as snakestone.
The women covered their flesh, the leaves
shook hands with the devil.
A song on the radio withered like grapes on the vine.
Trees hunkered down like old men
lighting cigars in the rain.
Someone sent a telegram to the sun saying:
Don't bother.
In its absence we ceased speaking
with the warmth of breath.
Everything went still and silent as a book
shelved in a closet. Everything
balanced on a simple white envelope.

DREAM OF AN OHIO OPERA

In the corner of an abandoned warehouse,
among the broken smiles
of windows, and radiators long since dormant,
an old, torn opera poster
is pasted to the wall beside me,
left long ago by students
or singers from some other time.
The female lead is dressed
like indistinct royalty, arms outstretched,
calling to the clouds above her.
What appears to be a golden fence
wraps around her crown,
leading, we presume, to a kingdom
long since departed.
Whatever music was here,
is now gone;
whatever story began,
must be continued elsewhere.
Outside, there is the stirring
of distant thunder, as if the sky
were remembering its own strength.
And I, with no response,
must take my leave.

A NOTE

Once, there was a golden age of letter writing, a time when the grand men and women of literature volleyed back and forth, ruminating on their art, their loves, their petty vendettas against the critics of the day. We bought tomes of their published epistles, mining for wisdom in the smallest asides. We believed in their intimacy, however much was by design. My words to you, my love, I keep closer than all of that. My words swim within the body and out, flicker between the leaves of trees, dangle from the hems of wayward clouds. I trust that you will know them when they arrive, and in your own way, respond in kind.

.

LULLABY

The last thing I hear of
the day, blessedly uneventful,
is your breathing, then
my own, a near-silence
rustling like wayward spirits
come too late;
the last movement
a whisper-thin branch of ash
tap-tapping against
dark, reflecting window,
deep fragrance of earth
beginning to stir within itself.
The fact of your warmth
when I come to bed,
my body chilled
from wandering the rooms
of self, is a book
not merely to be read,
but entered completely.

A SINGLE MAN

To love is to lose all
responsibility
of being upright.
One wants only to wallow,
to create more love
through sleep, through sex,
to take even one's meals
horizontally.
Today, I renounce love
completely, walk in
measured steps
toward no destination
at all.

THE POET

Sometimes he forgets where he has placed things, or what it was that he crossed the room to retrieve. Lets his whiskers grow into a white patch of bristle, small mice nesting in his ears. Sometimes he stares out of windows where others see nothing, stays at his desk for hours as if warding off a sickness. When he leaves, it is to collect the mail, should there be mail to collect; or for food and wine, should he be in need of these. He is often in need. You can see him coming a mile away. He has that word — that certain, indelible word — written all over him.

WHISKEY DAYS

Put the ice cubes in the cupboard, the credit cards in the freezer; fell asleep with one boot on, one boot off. No memory of the in-between hours, until they all become that way. In your dream, a mad woman is chasing you down, dressed only in a long coat the color of autumnal grass. One hole is worn at the elbow, flashing the thin white of the moon. Soon she will find your hiding place. Soon you will truly meet, and realize that you have both been more than just a little foolish.

LANDLOCKED

You would never know that the ocean exists, but for the affirmations of others, a postcard from a place where time is measured by the pull of tides. You would never know that the moon too is liquid, hydrological, a drum fit to burst. You would accept the wind as temporary and dry, like cigar smoke blown through the nostrils. You would drive through desert after desert, writing love poems in a worn, blue notebook, drinking whiskey as if it were the eternal substitute for water.

RED RIBBON

Red ribbon on the sidewalk,
shimmering
where no light could
have reached it.
I thought of you.
It was just one of those
types of nights.
My hand shifted from star
to tree, then back
as if on its own accord.
I could not, nor would not
dare to choose.
It was one of the last
types of nights this season.
And I thought of you.

Greg Watson is the author of eight collections of poetry, most recently *All the World at Once: New and Selected Poems*. He is also co-editor with Richard Broderick of *The Road by Heart: Poems of Fatherhood*, published by Nodin Press.

Connect with Greg

Instagram
@gregwatsonpoet

Other Titles
available at

www.amazon.com
and
www.NodinPress.com